D0005238

How to Improve Your Grammar

BY JESSICA DAVIDSON

87 30
425
DAV

Blairsville Junior High School
Blairsville, Pennsylvania

A Language Skills Concise Guide
FRANKLIN WATTS
New York | London | Toronto | Sydney | 1980

Library of Congress Cataloging in Publication Data

Davidson, Jessica.
How to improve your grammar.

(A Language skills concise guide)
Includes index.
SUMMARY: Discusses correct usage,
sentence structure, punctuation, and grammar.
Includes practice exercises with an answer key.
1. English language—Grammar—1950—
—Juvenile literature. [1. English language—Grammar]
I. Title. II. Series: Language skills concise guide.
PE1112.D28   428.2   80–15066
ISBN 0–531–04131–X

Copyright © 1980 by Jessica Davidson
All rights reserved
Printed in the United States of America
5 4 3 2

Contents

How to Improve Your Grammar

Chapter 1.
Dungarees in
the Courtroom

"Why do you wear the clothes you wear?"

"Because it's against the law to go without them."

"OK. Granted. But why do you wear the *particular* clothes you wear?"

"To keep warm. To keep dry. To protect my feet from broken glass."

Maybe. But that doesn't account for the type of shoes or the length of the skirt or the shade of the socks. Would mismatched socks keep your feet as warm and dry as socks of the same shade?

Admit it—you care about the impression you make on other people. Your clothing may be worn to keep you warm and dry, but it's worn for a lot of other reasons as well.

The same can be said about your language. You use language to ask questions and to communicate ideas, but that's not all.

Some people think of language as correct or incorrect and can always tell you which is which. But others prefer to think of three categories: formal and correct, informal, incorrect. Some ways of speaking and writing are just plain wrong.

(At no time is it proper to go outside dressed in your underwear—except perhaps to escape a fire!) Other ways of expressing yourself are acceptable, but only for informal speech and writing. (Dungarees are certainly acceptable in certain situations but not for a courtroom appearance or attendance at a graduation ceremony, a wedding, or a funeral.)

The dictionary makes this distinction by noting words or phrases as "colloquial" or "slang." Grammar books usually refer to this as "informal speech." Such usages are acceptable in the appropriate surroundings—in everyday conversation, in plays and movies, in friendly letters, in advertisements and commercials, but not in serious books, reports, or formal letters. Some languages actually have two kinds of vocabulary and grammar—spoken and written. English doesn't go that far, but the idea is there. Just as eating picnic-style is different from formal dining, formal and informal language are both acceptable in their respective surroundings. But it's never correct to bend down and slurp up the soup from the bowl or balance the peas on your knife.

When this book says that a usage is wrong, it means that to speak or write that way under any circumstance marks a person as uneducated or uninformed. Informal usage doesn't have that effect. In fact, using formally correct grammar all the time might seem as inappropriate as using a knife and fork to eat your hamburger at a picnic.

You're not likely to say "I aren't." You know that the correct form is "I am not" or "I'm not." But what happens when you turn the statement into a question?

Formal: Am I not?
Informal: Aren't I?

What's the answer to the question "Who's there?"

Formal: It is I.
Informal: It's me.

Strictly speaking, the informal answers above are incorrect.

But the formal versions are so stilted that almost no one uses them in friendly conversation.

A good but quite unanswerable question is this: How often must incorrect speech be used before it becomes acceptable in informal English? The language *does* change. Some usages once considered improper under any circumstance are now acceptable in informal speech. Should you feel free, then, to imitate poor usages that you hear?

Probably not. Many people squirm when they hear the language misused. Poor grammar might cost you that scholarship or job. Nobody will fault you for using correct English. So why take the chance?

Here are some very common examples of incorrect grammar. Maybe in ten years or so some of them will be acceptable in informal speech, but they aren't now. See if you can spot the errors below. Each sentence has one. On a separate piece of paper, write the sentences as they should be written. Then compare your sentences with those in the answer key.

1. This secret is just between you and I.
2. Us girls are the best players.
3. They act like they own the place.
4. My mother she works in the library.
5. What do you think of this here book?
6. Where did you hide it at?
7. That engine doesn't start like it should.
8. Speak slower.
9. He can't see too good.
10. I can't hardly hear you.
11. I don't know nothing about it.
12. Do you like to lay on the beach?
13. Leave him be.
14. The radio don't work.
15. My brother and myself will go to the fair.

The mistakes in sentences 1, 2, and 15 will be discussed under *pronouns* in Chapter 3. The mistakes in sentences 3 and 7 will be dealt with under *like and as* in the last chapter. The mistakes in sentences 4, 5, and 6 are redundancies; they contain extra, unneeded words. For these and for sentence 13, see in the last chapter the sections *this and that, let and leave.* Mistakes in sentences 8 and 9 result from a confusion between adjectives and adverbs. See Chapter 5 for help here. Sentences 10 and 11 are also discussed in Chapter 5— the problem of double negatives. You'll come to grips with *lay* and *lie* (sentence 12) in Chapter 4. Sentence 14 isn't discussed anywhere. But you probably recognized the mistake immediately.

This chapter and the last chapter in the book are about correct usage. All the others deal with how our language is put together: its sentence structure, punctuation, and grammar.

It's not really necessary to understand everything about a language in order to speak it correctly. You can drive a car without knowing anything about gears and levers. But such knowledge helps because it shows why things are the way they are. And things that make sense are easier to remember or keep straight.

Chapter 2.
Bits and Pieces–
The Sentence

WHAT IS A SENTENCE?

What's the shortest complete sentence in the English language? The answer may surprise you. The shortest sentence is two letters long. If you doubt it, read on.

First, of course, you have to know what a sentence is. You probably learned that a sentence is a group of words that expresses a complete thought. The definition becomes more useful, however, if this is added: A **sentence** is a group of words containing a **subject** and a **predicate**. The subject tells what person, place, thing, or idea the sentence is about —the **noun** or **pronoun**. The predicate always has a **verb** as its key word. No group of words can be a sentence unless the group contains a verb. The verb must be *expressed;* it cannot be *understood,* or implied.

There are two kinds of verbs, **action verbs** and **linking verbs.** Action verbs tell what the subject does or has had done to it: The mackerel *ate.* The mackerel *was eaten.* Linking verbs join the subject to descriptive words about the subject. The most usual linking verbs are parts of the verb "to be": *am, is, are, was, were, have been, should be,* etc. There are other linking verbs such as *seem, sound,* and *taste.* Here are some examples of sentences with linking verbs: Elephants *are* large. The dinner *smells* delicious.

A brief statement that is a sentence would be something like *Birds fly.* On a diagram it looks like this:

Subject	Predicate
birds	fly

But there is one kind of sentence—a **command**—in which the subject is understood to be the person spoken to. "Get ready!" means "You, get ready!" "Get set!" means "You, get set!" And so the shortest English sentence is, of course, "Go!" On a diagram, it looks like this:

Subject	Predicate
(you)	go

"Quiet!" is a command, but it is not a sentence. It is a fragment that stands for the full sentence, "You, be quiet!" While the subject ("you") can be understood, the verb ("be") cannot. Every sentence must have a verb. "Quiet!" doesn't.

Check your understanding of what a sentence is by setting up two columns on your paper: Write *subject* on the left, *predicate* on the right. If the group of words is a sentence, you should be able to break it into the two parts. If it isn't, complete the sentence by adding in parentheses whatever is needed to complete it. To make certain that you have a noun or pronoun and a verb, underline them.

Examples:

	Subject	Predicate
1. The dogs are barking.	the <u>dogs</u>	<u>are</u> barking
2. The barking dogs.	the barking <u>dogs</u>	(<u>annoyed</u> me)

Here are the groups of words to try:

a. Never saw a purple cow.
b. A splendid piece of work.

c. Go home.
d. He eats too much.
e. Never say die.

FINDING THE SUBJECT

Subjects usually come at the beginning of the sentence, but this is not always the case. The following two sentences say exactly the same thing and on a diagram would show subject and predicate in exactly the same way:

A growling dog ran out of the house.
Out of the house ran a growling dog.

subject	*predicate*
a growling dog	ran out of the house

How do you tell? Find the verb first. You might think that the verb is *growling* but it isn't. The sentence *A brown dog ran out of the house* has exactly the same form. What action took place and what word shows it? The only verb in that sentence is *ran.* To find the subject, ask yourself, what ran? It wasn't the house, that's clear.

Deal with the following sentences in the same way. Find the **simple predicate,** the verb, first. Then ask who or what performed the action to find the one word that is the **simple subject.** List the simple subject and simple predicate on your paper. For the growling dog sentence, your paper would show:

ss	*sp*
dog	ran

What will it show for these?
1. Long ago, in the days of knights and dragons, men fought with spears and lances.
2. Time after time, with enormous patience, the little red squirrel tried unsuccessfully to gnaw its way out of the steel cage.

So far we've been considering two kinds of sentences: statements (formally named **declarative sentences**) and commands (formally named **imperative sentences**). There are two other kinds: **interrogative sentences** (questions) and **exclamatory sentences** (exclamations). In these kinds of sentences, you will find the subject and predicate in unusual positions. To find the simple subject and the simple predicate, answer the question with a simple statement. For example, answer the question "Has Donna returned?" with the statement "Donna has returned." Then it's clear:

$$ss \qquad\qquad sp$$

Donna	has returned

Turn "What a beautiful cake she baked!" into the statement "She baked a beautiful cake." Then the diagram looks like this:

$$ss \qquad sp$$

she	baked

COMPOUND SUBJECTS
AND PREDICATES

Not all sentences have simple subjects and simple predicates. Some have **compound subjects:**

Juniors and seniors attended the dance.

Some have **compound predicates:**

Chris washed and waxed the car.

Some have both:

Jack and Jill found the dog and brought it home.

COMPOUND SENTENCES

Some sentences consist of two simple sentences joined by the conjunctions *and, but,* or *or*. This combination is called a **compound sentence.** The two parts of a compound sentence are of equal weight. Neither one depends on the other. If you put a period (full-stop) in place of the conjunction you would have two short sentences:

> We waited for two hours, and
> we telephoned every ten minutes.

> We waited for two hours.
> We telephoned every ten minutes.

COMPLEX SENTENCES

Another type of sentence is called a **complex sentence.** Complex sentences resemble compound sentences, but they are connected by special conjunctions called **subordinating conjunctions.** These are some of the most frequently used subordinating conjunctions:

after	although	as if	as long as
because	before	if	since
unless	until	whenever	while

In a complex sentence, one part is the main part while the other part is the subordinate part. The subordinate part explains or qualifies the main part. If you take out the conjunction and put in a period, as you did in the compound sentences above, you would still have two simple sentences but they wouldn't make good sense. Something would seem to be missing. Here's an example.

Complex sentence
Elizabeth left the party before Charlie arrived.
Complex sentence split into two sentences
Elizabeth left the party. Charlie arrived.

Do you see what happened? The connection between the two thoughts that gave them a specific meaning is lost.

How do you tell which is the **main clause** of a complex sentence and which is the **subordinate clause?** First, by using common sense. What is the main idea that the writer wants to tell you? A more mechanical and perhaps surer way is to look for the subordinating conjunction. It is always the first word of the subordinate clause.

Notice also that the main clause is always a sentence. The subordinate clause, with its conjunction in place, is not a sentence even though it has a subject and a verb. Subordinating clauses are sentence fragments.

In stories written for young children, most sentences are short and simple. Adults can get quite bored by reading such writing. That's why writers for older readers frequently use compound and complex sentences.

But watch out! Compound and complex sentences both need conjunctions. When you are writing, never just string a group of sentences together without using conjunctions. If you do, you'll have run-on sentences:

Run-on sentence
> I don't want to look for clothes on Saturday the shops are too crowded you have to wait so long for help.

Corrected form
> I don't want to look for clothes on Saturday. The shops are too crowded. You have to wait so long for help.

Also correct
> I don't want to look for clothes on Saturday because the shops are too crowded and you have to wait so long for help.

Now let's see what you've learned so far. There are eight sentences below. Some are simple sentences with compound subjects or compound predicates. Some are compound sentences. Some are complex sentences. See if you can sort them out. Write your answers—*compound subject, com-*

pound predicate, or *complex sentence*—on a separate sheet of paper, but don't check the answer key just yet.

1. If I had known how good the dessert would be, I wouldn't have eaten so much bread.
2. My friend George and my brother have gone to the show.
3. The home team won the last game of the season and became the regional champions.
4. They intended to climb to the top of the mountain but they were too tired.
5. I won't let you go unless you promise that you'll come back.
6. The basketball team and the football team are planning a joint picnic.
7. You'd better apologize or I'll never speak to you again.
8. Since you're waiting at the counter anyway, will you buy me a soda?

You should have found three complex sentences. They are numbers 1, 5, and 8. Can you find the main clause in each? Remember that the main clause is the one that tells what really happened. Write down on your paper the first two or three words of the main clause and the first two or three words of the subordinate clause so you can check your answers.

Did you find the two compound sentences? In each, copy the conjunction and the two words that follow it.

There are two sentences with compound subjects. What are these compound subjects?

Finally, there is one sentence with a compound predicate. What are the two verbs of this compound predicate?

Now check the answer key.

Chapter 3.
You Name It—
Nouns and Pronouns

NOUNS AND THEIR USES

Suppose you were teaching English to a foreign student whose language you didn't know. Generally speaking, you could teach the student nouns by pointing to what was named. The exceptions would be the nouns that name ideas like justice, feelings like joy, and activities like carpentry and tennis.

There are two kinds of nouns—**proper nouns** and **common nouns.** The proper nouns are always capitalized. They are the names of particular persons, places, or things. Common nouns name a *type* of person, place, or thing. *Jane Fonda, Chicago,* and *Toyota* are proper nouns that correspond to the common nouns *actress, city,* and *car.*

Nouns are used, as we have seen, as the subject of a sentence:

$$s. \qquad p.$$

$$\underline{\text{dogs} \mid \text{bark}}$$

They are also used as the **direct object** of a verb—the

person, place, or thing that receives the action of a verb. This is how the diagram of a direct object looks:

s.   *v.*   *d.o.*

dogs | eat | meat

They are used, in addition, as **subject complements**—words that define or describe the subject. The diagram of a subject complement looks like this:

s.   *v.*   *s.c.*

dogs | are \ mammals

Finally, nouns can also be used as **indirect objects.** In the sentence "Dad gave the dogs bones," the noun *bones* is the direct object because *bones* are what Dad gave. *Dogs* is the indirect object because he gave the bones *to* the dogs. The word "to" is always understood before an indirect object. The sentence really means "Dad gave bones to the dogs." More will be said about this in Chapter 6, but here's what the diagram looks like:

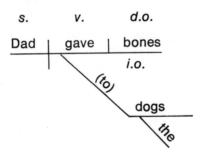

(The placement of the word "the" will be explained in Chapter 5.)

    See if you can pick out the *subjects, complements, direct objects,* and *indirect objects* in the following sentences. You may want to set up your paper in columns with the italicized words as headings. Or, you may find it more challenging to diagram the sentences, using the following patterns:

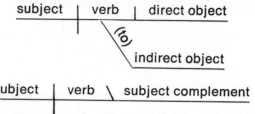

In the answer key, both groups of answers are shown.

1. Athletes win medals.
2. Athletes are celebrities.
3. Policemen give speeders tickets.
4. Dogs chase squirrels.

PERSONAL PRONOUNS

Why is it important to know whether a noun is being used as subject, subject complement, or direct or indirect object? In some languages—Latin, for instance—it is absolutely necessary to know this because the form of the noun changes from one use to another. In English this doesn't happen to nouns, but it does happen to almost all the **personal pronouns.**

All the personal pronouns except *it* and *you* function as either subjects or as objects, but not both. They are *not* interchangeable. *It* and *you* are interchangeable.

The following personal pronouns can be used only as subjects or as subject complements:

I   he   she   we   they

The following personal pronouns can be used only as objects:

me   him   her   us   them

Few English-speaking people over the age of three are likely to say "Me want to eat" or "Him want to eat." Yet when two pronouns are joined to form a compound subject

(14)

many people wrongly say, "Him and me want to eat" or "Him and I want to eat." If the pronouns don't work separately, they won't work together. On the basic sentence diagram, subject | predicate, subject pronouns can appear only on the lefthand side.

The use of pronouns as objects is just as troublesome. No one would say "Mother called I," yet some people wrongly say "Mother called George and I." Object pronouns may be used only as the direct or indirect object of a verb or as the object of a preposition. Again, if the pronouns don't work separately, they won't work together.

Subject complements present a different situation. Here a real difference between formal and informal language occurs. Formal language demands a subject pronoun: "It is I." But just about everyone says "It's me" in informal speech. "It is we" would sound really strange, though it is the formally correct way to say what we mean when we say "It's us."

Watch what happens, though, when the sentence is longer: "It is I who am to blame." Try to put "me" into that sentence. Sounds ridiculous, doesn't it?

For practice in writing formal English, copy these sentences on your paper, filling in each blank with one of the pronouns in parentheses.

1. It is ———— (he, him) who is the loser.
2. The teacher promised ———— (her, she) and ————
   (I, me) that we could be captains.
3. It was ———— (they, them) who discovered the secret.
4. Please give Chris and ———— (I, me) another chance.
5. It was ———— (she, her) who was elected president.

If you enjoy filling in diagrams, you may find them especially helpful in choosing the correct pronoun. Subject pronouns can go only in the spots marked below by single asterisks:

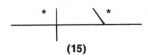

(15)

Object pronouns can go only in the spots marked below by double asterisks:

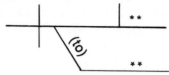

Where there is a compound subject or a compound object the diagram shows it this way:

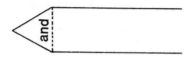

The sentence "You and I gave him and her the money" would look like this on a diagram:

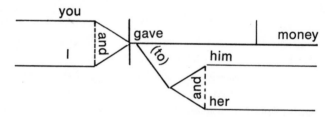

You might like to try putting these sentences into diagram form to help you decide which of the pronouns in parentheses to choose:

1. _____ (He, Him) and _____ (I, me) ate the chocolate.
2. The principal gave _____ (they, them) and _____ (we, us) certificates.
3. _____ (She, Her) and _____ (he, him) phoned Joe and _____ (I, me).

POSSESSIVE PRONOUNS

Another tricky group of pronouns is the group known as the **possessive pronouns.** Nouns show possession by adding an *'s* or an *s'*: a *dog's* collar, *girls'* dresses. Pronouns do not use apostrophes. The *dog's* collar is *its* collar, not *it's* collar. *It's* means "it is." It does not mean "belonging to it." When possessive pronouns are used with nouns, these are the forms: *my, your, his, her, its, our,* and *their:*

> This is *my* book. *Your* book is missing.

When possessive pronouns are used as subjects in place of nouns, subject complements, or objects, these are the forms: *mine, yours, his, hers, its, ours,* and *theirs:*

> *Mine* is the red one. Is this book *yours?* They lost *theirs* so we gave them *ours.*

COMPOUND PRONOUNS

Compound pronouns are formed by adding *-self* or *-selves* to personal pronouns. Sometimes these compound pronouns are used to intensify or emphasize the pronoun:

> **They themselves are to blame.**

Sometimes they are used as objects of verbs or prepositions:

> He washed himself.
> She gave herself a shampoo.
> I can do it by myself.

In these cases they are called **reflexive pronouns** because they refer (*reflect*) back to the subject.

Notice that some of the reflexive pronouns are formed from object pronouns and some are formed from possessive pronouns. On your paper divide this list in two columns to show the two groups:

> myself   yourself   himself   herself   itself
> ourselves   themselves

In which group does *herself* belong? What logic is there in the formation of these compound pronouns that can tell us that *herself* is formed from the object pronoun *her* and not from the possessive pronoun *her?* Notice that it is part of the group of third-person pronouns: *himself, herself, itself, themselves.* First-person pronouns (*I, we*) and second-person pronouns (*you*) add the ending to the possessive form.

The only reason for stressing this is that some people don't recognize this and say *hisself* and *theirselves.* The language might have developed that way, but it didn't. Always remember: *hisself* and *theirselves* are never correct.

Also remember that these *-self* pronouns must always refer to another word in the same sentence. It is incorrect to say "The teacher gave the assignment to Jean and myself" or "Himself and his brother are coming." The pronouns should be *me* and *he.*

Would you be surprised to learn that there are four *more* kinds of pronouns still to come? There are the **indefinite pronouns,** words like *each, anyone,* and *some*—there are too many to list here. These will be discussed in the next chapter because the main trouble they cause concerns what verb to use with them. In that chapter you will also find the **demonstrative pronouns**—*this, that, these,* and *those*—for the same reason. The last two groups, the **relative pronouns** (*who, whom, which, what, that, whoever,* etc.) and the **interrogative pronouns** (*who, whom, which,* and *what*) cause very little trouble. The problems of *who* and *whom* and of *who, that,* and *which* are dealt with in the last chapter.

Chapter 4.
Where the Action Is
–Verbs

ACTION VERBS
AND LINKING VERBS

The first chapter pointed out that there are two basic kinds of verbs, action and linking. The best known of the linking verbs is *be* (or any of its parts). When a linking verb is used, it is easy to see that no action is involved. In the sentence "Your name is Jane," nothing happens. Tarzan's version, "You Jane," says the same thing, though ungrammatically. But how can words like *smell, taste, feel,* and *appear* be linking verbs?

Surely smelling is an activity. Yes, but only sometimes. It depends on how the verb is used. In the sentence "The dog smells his dinner," the dog is certainly active. But in the sentence "The stew smells good," it's equally clear that the stew is not going around sniffing.

One easy way to tell whether a verb is used as an action or a linking verb is to substitute some part of the verb *be* for it. If it makes sense, the verb is a linking verb. "The stew is good" makes sense. "The dog is his dinner" doesn't. Now try to substitute some verb that is clearly and always an action verb. "The dog eats his dinner." It works.

Number your paper from one to eleven. Write the verb that you find in each sentence below. Then write *action* or *linking* next to it, and note down a verb you could substitute for that verb and still have the sentence make sense.

1. Please *remain* after class to discuss this.
2. What actually happened *remains* a mystery.
3. The water *tastes* peculiar.
4. Most cooks *taste* the batter before baking it.
5. She *seems* strong enough for the job.
6. I hope this gadget *proves* useful.
7. The cat's fur *feels* very soft.
8. Did you *feel* the cat's fur?
9. Can you *prove* your answer?
10. Marcie *looks* at the scrapbook.
11. Your work *looks* very good.

Of course, used differently and in other contexts, some of the italicized words above may not be verbs at all; they may be nouns. Is *smell* a verb or a noun? It can be either. There are many words like this, words that are able to serve either as nouns or verbs. For the sentences below, write on your paper one word that will fill both blanks in each pair. Then label the word V. or N. to show which is the noun and which is the verb.

Example: (a) I won't ———— the clams.
　　　　　(b) I don't like the ———— of clams.

　　　　　Answer: taste　a. V.　b. N.

1. (a) He won't ———— about school on the weekends.
　 (b) His ———— on the subject of snakes was interesting.
2. (a) My friends are ———— in the pool.
　 (b) ———— is the summer sport I like best.
3. (a) Who is taking you to the ————?
　 (b) Shall we ———— to the jukebox music?
4. (a) I ———— to school every day.
　 (b) It's a long ————.

5. (a) If it's too heavy to lift, I'll _____ you.
   (b) Thanks, but I don't need any _____.

TRANSITIVE AND INTRANSITIVE VERBS

Verbs can be divided into groups in yet another way depending on how they are used. They can be **transitive** or **intransitive.** Transitive verbs act upon something; they have direct objects. Intransitive verbs do not.

Some verbs, like *blush, lie, sneeze,* and *snicker,* can be used only as intransitive verbs. They do not act upon anything and so they never have a direct object. Some verbs, like *lay, raise, hit,* and *blame,* can be used only as transitive verbs. They must have a direct object. You *raise* something, you *hit* something, you *blame* someone or something, you *lay* your books on the desk. But most verbs are transitive in some sentences, intransitive in others: The children are *playing* (intransitive). They are *playing* softball (transitive). Your dictionary will show this as *vi* and *vt.*

Use each of the following verbs in two sentences, first intransitively then transitively. The answers in the answer key are only suggestions; your answers need not match them. Here are the verbs: *bite, sing, wash, win, run.*

AUXILIARY, OR HELPING, VERBS

A small but very important group of verbs forms the category of **auxiliary,** or **helping, verbs,** so-called because they help out another verb. These are the most common auxiliary verbs:

> be (am, is, are, was, were, been)
> have (has, had)
> shall should
> can could
> will would
> do (did, does)
> may might
> must

When these auxiliary verbs are joined to main verbs, the entire phrase forms the simple predicate. In the sentence "He must have been dreaming," the *verb,* not the *verbs,* is "must have been dreaming."

PRINCIPAL PARTS OF VERBS

There are two forms of **regular verbs**—verbs that follow usual patterns—in the present tense, the tense that shows what is happening now. You can write either *he walks* or *he is walking.* Generally we use *he walks* to mean what he ordinarily does: I ride the bus to school but he walks. We use *he is walking* to mean that that is what he is doing this very minute. *Walks* is the **simple present.** *Is walking* is called the **present participle.**

The past tense has three basic forms: she *walked* (**simple past**); she *was walking* (**continuing past**); and she *has walked* (**past participle**). Thus, regular verbs add the suffix *-ing* to show the present participle. They add *-ed* to show the simple past and the past participle. The forms of the verb are called its **principal parts.** For regular verbs, the principal parts look like this:

walk   walking   walked   walked

The basic form of the verb does not change to show the future tense. In this way English is different from many other languages. To show the future we use the helping verbs *shall* and *will.*

IRREGULAR VERBS

There are many **irregular verbs.** Like regular verbs, they all add *-ing* for the present participle, but for the past and the past participle there are many unexpected changes. Some verbs change the vowels:

sing   singing   sang   (has) sung

Some change the vowels and use -*en* instead of -*ed* for the past participle:

break   breaking   broke   (has) broken

Some change the basic verb completely:

go   going   went   (has) gone
buy   buying   bought   (has) bought

A very few make no change at all for the past and past participle:

set   setting   set   (has) set
burst   bursting   burst   (has) burst

The dictionary usually lists principal parts that differ from the regular form. In some dictionaries, nothing is listed if the principal parts are all regular. To see what your dictionary does, look up some words you're sure of such as *walk, teach,* and *sing.*

Check to see whether you know the principal parts of some common verbs. Head your paper this way:

present   present participle   past   past participle
(am _____ing)   (have _____)

You are going to fill in the columns using the words below, being especially careful of the spelling of the present participle. In some cases, you will have to decide whether the final consonant of the basic verb is to be doubled (set—setting, but beat—beating) or whether a final *e* should be dropped (shake—shaking, but dye—dyeing).

There are no answers in the answer key for this exercise because practice in using your dictionary for this purpose is important.

Now here are the verbs:

dive   wring   drown   lie   drink   fly   lay   freeze

hit	speak	forget	sting	write	throw	beat	shake
dye	sleep	steal	bring	drive	begin	ride	forgive

USING PAST OR PAST PARTICIPLE

Now that you know or at least know how to find the principal parts of irregular verbs, make sure that you know how to use them. In the following sentences choose the correct form—past or past participle—to fill the blank. On your paper, write the complete verb for each sentence (*has gone,* not just *gone,* for example). Then check your answers with those in the answer key.

1. It has _____ much colder since morning. (become)
2. School _____ last week. (begin)
3. Have you ever _____ a minibike? (ride)
4. Has she _____ that car before? (drive)
5. The hurricane _____ destruction to the countryside. (bring)
6. When she apologized, I _____ her. (forgive)
7. That cat has _____ every bit of our food! (steal)
8. Has the baby _____ his milk? (drink)
9. She _____ the ball up in the air. (throw)
10. The birds have _____ from the nest. (fly)

LIE AND LAY

The two irregular verbs that cause the most trouble are *lie* and *lay.* Probably the difficulty arises, at least in part, because the present tense of *lay* is the same as the past tense of *lie.* Look at the principal parts of both verbs. To *lie* is to rest. (We're ignoring the other verb to *lie,* which means to tell a falsehood.) To *lay* is to place.

present	*present participle*	*past*	*past participle*
lie—lies	(are) lying	lay	(have) lain
lay—lays	(are) laying	laid	(have) laid

The verb to *lie* is intransitive. It cannot have an object. The verb to *lay* is transitive. It must have an object. You cannot say "He lays down" any more than you can say "He places down." He *lies* down. He *lays the book* down.

Number your paper 1 to 10 and write in the missing part of *lie* or *lay*. If the verb has an object, copy the object next to the verb.

Example: He _____ the blankets on the bed.
You should write: laid the blankets.

1. Gather up those papers. Don't leave them _____ around.
2. You may _____ your coat on the bed.
3. My mother can't come to the phone; she's _____ down.
4. When the last snow melted, I found the rusty shovel. It had _____ on the ground all winter.
5. I can't find my car keys. I thought I had _____ them on the dresser.
6. The hen _____ two eggs yesterday.
7. Do you let your dog _____ on the sofa?
8. I fell asleep five minutes after I _____ down.
9. Yesterday the mayor _____ the cornerstone for the town hall.
10. Now I _____ me down to sleep.

SINGULAR OR PLURAL VERB

Verbs have to agree with their subjects. The word "agree" is used in the same sense as in the sentence "Pickles don't agree with me." With regular verbs this presents very little difficulty. Some irregular verbs have a greater variety of forms in the present tense and cause more trouble.

The real problem concerning agreement of subject and verb comes in identifying whether the subject is singular or plural:

Each of the boys (deserves, deserve) a medal.

The subject is *each,* which stands for *each one.* This is singular. *Deserves* is correct.

A singular pronoun in the subject must match up with a singular pronoun later in the sentence:

Each of the boys deserves *his* medal.

This is easier to see if you rewrite the sentence this way:

Each one of the boys deserves *his* medal.

Their medal wouldn't make sense, since each got a medal. They didn't share a medal.

Each is an indefinite pronoun. The most familiar indefinite pronouns that are always singular are:

anybody   anyone   anything   somebody
someone   something   everybody   everyone
everything   nobody   no one   nothing
each   either   neither   another

Of the demonstrative pronouns, *this* and *that* are always singular.

There are some indefinite pronouns that are sometimes singular, sometimes plural, depending upon the sense in which they are used. Look carefully:

Some of the people *are* German.
Some of the text *is* missing.

Are any of the questions easy?
Is any of the cake left?

Most of the lights *are* out.
Most of the work *is* done.

None of the guides *speak* English.
None of this *makes* sense.

These are tricky to decide. Your decision has to be based

on meaning. If you can replace the pronoun with a number such as five, for example, the pronoun obviously stands for more than one and therefore needs a plural form of the verb. If you can replace the pronoun with the words "a part," a singular form of the verb is called for.

Some indefinite pronouns are always plural:

many   several   few   both

Choose the correct word for each blank and write the complete sentences on your paper:

1. Each of the cats _____ (is, are) going to catch a mouse for _____ (its, their) dinner.
2. Neither of the men _____ (wants, want) to change _____ (his, their) vote.
3. Will either of the girls give up _____ (her, their) place in the line?
4. One of the books _____ (has, have) been moved from _____ (its, their) proper place on the shelf.
5. Some of the books _____ (has, have) been shortened for _____ (its, their) reprinting in the *Reader's Digest.*

HIS OR HER

What do you do when a pronoun such as *each, everyone,* or *no one* applies to both men and women?

No one likes to admit (his, her) mistakes.

Until recently, it was acceptable to say "No one likes to admit *his* mistakes," and the pronoun *his* was understood to include everybody. In sayings such as "Man does not live by bread alone," *man* was understood to mean human beings of both sexes. But recently there has been much dissatisfaction with the use of male pronouns to include women. That is why in formal writing nowadays you will often find *his or her* instead of just *his.* The sentence may read "No one likes to admit his or her mistakes."

It is sometimes possible to recast a sentence to avoid the awkwardness and the problem altogether:

People do not like to admit their mistakes.

In informal speech, it is becoming acceptable to say "No one likes to admit *their* mistakes." Wrong? Yes. But no worse than saying "Aren't I?"

Chapter 5.
Which? What kind?
How many? How?
Where? When?—
Adjectives and Adverbs

MODIFIERS

Nouns tell you what you're talking about. Verbs tell what the nouns did or had done to them. Adjectives and adverbs answer the questions shown in the title of this chapter. They are **modifiers.** They modify, or change, meaning.

Consider this sentence:

Dogs attack cats.

See how it is modified when adjectives and adverbs are added:

Fierce dogs often attack large cats.
Timid dogs never attack friendly cats.

The basic sentence—the simple subject and simple predicate—remains the same, but the meaning has certainly been modified.

What happens to the diagram when these modifiers are added? This is the basic diagram:

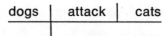

In sentences with action verbs, the modifiers always appear on slanted lines directly below the words they modify. The words that modify nouns are **adjectives.** Those that modify verbs, adjectives, and other adverbs are **adverbs.** The diagrams look like this:

dogs | attack | cats   dogs | attack | cats
  fierce   often   large   timid   never   friendly

The diagrams clearly show that *fierce, large, timid,* and *friendly* are adjectives, while *often* and *never* are adverbs.

ADJECTIVES

Most adjectives are descriptive: *good, huge, noisy.* Some are just demonstrative; they tell which one: *this, that, these, those.* Some are numerical: *one, twenty, fifth.* The **articles—** *a, an,* and *the*—are adjectives. Words we've met as possessive pronouns and indefinite pronouns can also be used as adjectives: *my* hat, *some* books. Finally, there are interrogative adjectives: *Which* hat? *Whose* books?

Adjectives are often used as subject complements:

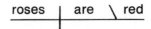

roses | are \ red

Except for this situation, adjectives will always be found on slanted lines below the nouns they modify.

ADVERBS

Adverbs tell where, when, or how the action of the verb occurs. *Not* is an adverb that tells whether it occurs at all. Some few adverbs answer the question "To what extent?" These are the only adverbs that do not modify verbs. They modify adjectives or other adverbs: a *very* good dinner. To what extent good? *Very.*

This is the way such adverbs appear on a diagram:

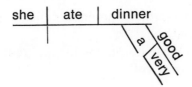

Here is an adverb modifying another adverb:

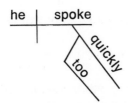

You cannot always tell from a diagram what the word order of a sentence is, but you can always tell which words are the modifiers. By their placement beside nouns or verbs, you can also tell whether they are adjectives or adverbs. These three sentences would all be diagramed in exactly the same way:

Patiently the bedraggled little dog waited outside.
Outside the bedraggled little dog waited patiently.
The bedraggled little dog waited patiently outside.

This is the diagram:

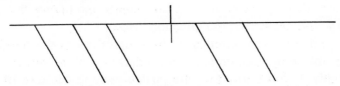

Make a copy of it on your paper and see how the words fit in. Always start to fill in a diagram by placing the simple subject and the simple predicate in position.

The above diagram can also be used for these two sentences:

The tearful, frightened children scurried
quietly upstairs.
Did those horrid, menacing creatures
go away yet?

Some adjectives and adverbs are closely related. Many adverbs are formed by adding the suffix -*ly* to the adjective:

A *conscientious* student works *conscientiously.*

Only those adverbs that are derived directly from adjectives will end in -*ly.*

There are many other adverbs of time (*yesterday, now, never*), place (*inside, nowhere, here*), and degree (*more, very, somewhat*) that have no connection with adjectives. Also there are many words ending in -*ly* that are not adverbs: *lovely, friendly, rely, tally,* for example. But the sight of -*ly* at a word's end is one indication that the word might be an adverb. Almost always, the adverbs that answer the question "How?" end in -*ly.*

Be quiet! Work quietly! Both commands are grammatically correct. Do you see why? How would you show this on a diagram? Check your diagrams with those in the answer key.

Quiet is a subject complement. Since *be* is a linking verb, the adjective modifies the subject *you,* which is understood. *Quietly,* of course, is an adverb, modifying the verb *work* and answering the question "How?"

For practice, identify all the adjectives and adverbs in the following sentences and indicate which words they modify. If you agree that the easiest way to be sure of this is to place the sentences on diagrams, do it that way. Otherwise show your answers in columns. Both methods are illustrated in the example and given in the answer key.

Example: That very intelligent child solved the difficult problem rather quickly.

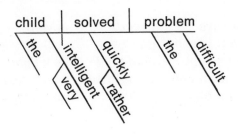

adj.	modifying noun	adverb modifying adjective
that	child	very intelligent
intelligent	child	*modifying verb*
the	problem	quickly solved
difficult	problem	*modifying adverb*
		rather quickly

Here are the sentences to work with:
1. Those skimpy portions seem exceptionally small.
2. That nearly dead battery will never start my old car.
3. His very valuable violin almost always makes lovely music.

SPECIAL ADVERBS

A few adverbs that do not add -*ly* but keep the same form as their matching adjectives have become familiar in expressions. These are very special cases. They look like adjectives but they are adverbs and would sound positively strange if -*ly* were added:

go *slow*	do it *right*	don't come *late*
hold *tight*	throw it *high*	he can't see *straight*
come *close*	run *fast*	hit *hard* stand *near*

In some cases, however, adverbs are formed from these

adjectives by adding -*ly*, but the new adverbs have somewhat different meanings. Consider these:

adjective	*adverb*	*adverb*
a *slow* speed	go *slow*	walk *slowly*
a *tight* knot	hold *tight*	tie it *tightly*
a *close* friend	come *close*	watch *closely*
a *hard* ball	hit *hard*	he *hardly* knew me

GOOD AND WELL

This brings us to the problem of *good* and *well*. If you forgot that verbs like *taste* and *smell* are linking verbs, you might think that in the sentence "The ice cream tastes good," *good* modifies *tastes.* It doesn't. It modifies *ice cream,* exactly as in the sentence "The ice cream is good." *Well* is the adverb that pairs up with the adjective *good. Good* players play *well.*

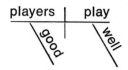

The problem is that the word *well* has another meaning—"in good health." In that meaning, it's an adjective. That's why both these sentences are correct:

| I | feel | \ good | | I | feel | \ well |

They are slightly different in meaning. In the first sentence a certain feeling of pleasure and satisfaction is expressed. The second sentence says merely, "I don't feel sick."

The opposite of "I feel good" is "I feel bad." (If you feel *badly,* it's because your sense of touch is poor, and you can't tell by feeling the cloth whether it's silk or canvas.) The opposite of "I feel well" is "I feel unwell" or "I feel sick."

NEGATIVES

While we're dealing with problem adverbs, consider the negative adverbs like *not, never, nowhere,* and *hardly.* You can't use two of them together and you can't use them with negative pronouns like *nobody* and *nothing.* You may understand a person who says "I never said nothing," but, strictly speaking, this means "There never was a time when I kept my mouth shut; I always had something to say."

One negative is enough. Two are too many. Rewrite these sentences correctly on your paper. Those marked with an asterisk * can be corrected in two ways. Write both versions, as in the example.

Example: Incorrect: I didn't go nowhere.
Correct: I didn't go anywhere.
or
I went nowhere.

* 1. I don't know no one here.
* 2. They don't know nothing about it.
  3. The newborn colt can't barely stand up.
* 4. We didn't have no money.
  5. I can't hardly hear you.
  6. She never told nobody.

COMPARATIVES AND SUPERLATIVES

TV commercials are forever assuring you that some product makes your teeth whiter or your breath fresher or your shirts cleaner and brighter, but they seldom tell you whiter than *what,* fresher than *what,* etc. *Whiter, fresher, cleaner,* and *brighter* are the **comparative forms** of the adjectives. The form is called comparative because it is designed to compare two things. This star is *brighter* than that one.

Most short adjectives form the comparative by adding *-er.* Most long adjectives use the adverb *more* instead: *more economical,* for example. Never use both *more* and the *-er* ending together. *More sweeter* is incorrect English.

Adverbs ending in the suffix *-ly* use *more* to form the comparative: *more quickly,* not *quicklier.*

To compare three or more things, or to say that something is the best of all possible things, use the **superlative form:** the *whitest* of the three, the *most economical* of all, she works *most efficiently.*

Comparisons can also be made in the opposite direction: *less beautiful, least attractive.*

A few common adjectives and adverbs change their form completely when used for comparison:

modifier	comparative	superlative
good	better	best
bad	worse	worst
much	more	most
many	more	most
little	less	least
few	less	least

Copy these sentences on your paper, filling the blanks with the correct comparative or superlative form of the word in italics.

1. Both girls are *tall,* but Janice is the _____ of the two.
2. Today's weather was *bad,* but yesterday's was _____ than today's, and Sunday's was the _____ of the week.
3. I'm a *good* speller, but Chris is _____ than I, and Dale is the _____ in the class.
4. My brother has very *little* money, but I have even _____ than he does, and my sister has the _____ of all of us.
5. The worm crawls *slowly,* but the turtle crawls _____ than the worm, and the snail crawls _____ of all.

Chapter 6.
Trying to Tell It to You—
Prepositional Phrases,
Infinitives, and
Participles

PREPOSITIONAL PHRASES

At the turn of the century, schools used to require their pupils to memorize a list of prepositions in alphabetical order. My mother used to recite them to me as if they were a nursery rhyme. Here is how the list begins: *aboard, about, above, across, after, against, along, amid* or *amidst, among* or *amongst, around, at, athwart; before, behind, below, beside* or *besides, between* or *betwixt, beyond, by; during. . . .*

Get the idea? And by far the most common prepositions are those we haven't even reached yet in the alphabetical listing: *for, from, in, of, to,* and *with.*

Prepositions always have objects: about *birds.* The objects may have modifiers: in *the southern* sky. This is how they are placed on a diagram:

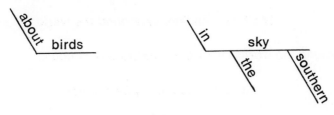

The preposition with its object and modifiers is called a **prepositional phrase.** Prepositional phrases can be used either as adjectives or as adverbs, because they answer the same questions: Which one? What kind? Where? When? How? That is why in the diagram they are placed like adjectives and adverbs, with the preposition itself on the line that the adjective or adverb would usually occupy, like this:

The boy in the back row was doodling with his red pencil.

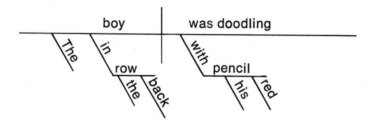

Name the prepositional phrases in these sentences. If you enjoy diagrams, draw three like the one above on your paper and place the following sentences on them:

1. The crew of the sinking ship scrambled aboard the remaining lifeboats.
2. The fence around the old playground was destroyed by the heavy storm.
3. The principal of the middle school was pleased with our artistic display.

Like adverbs, prepositional phrases can modify adjectives and other adverbs:

Their work is famous *around the world.*

Around the world tells *where* the work is famous.

He will speak today *before noon.*

Before noon modifies or explains *what part of* today is meant. This is how the diagrams look:

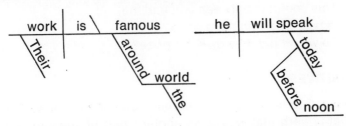

Find the prepositional phrases in these sentences and tell what they modify. You might like to try making up your own diagrams for them.

4.   He is playing outside in the rain.
5.   Sit here beside me.
6.   She is hungry for news of him.

Prepositions always have objects. It follows that the word on a diagram that appears following a preposition is always an object. Go back, now, to the only part of speech where it is important to know whether the word is a subject or an object—the pronoun, because the form of a pronoun changes.

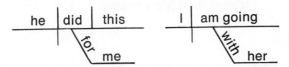

Those pronouns that can be used only as subject pronouns —*I, he, she, we,* and *they*—can never appear after a preposition.

When a preposition has a compound object it looks like this on the diagram:

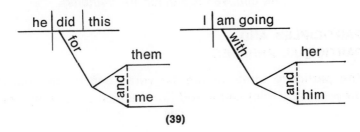

(39)

Make your own diagrams for these sentences:

1. This secret is between you and me.
2. Is he going with them or us?
3. To whom did they give the prize?

INFINITIVES

The word *to* isn't always a preposition. Often it is part of a verbal (a verb that serves as another part of speech) called an **infinitive.** *To walk, to think, to be* are infinitives.

Infinitives can be used as nouns, as adjectives, and as adverbs. As nouns, they can be either subjects, subject complements, or objects. Here are some examples:

> *To know* her is *to love* her.
> (subject and subject complement)

> We wanted *to eat.*
> (object of verb)

> He is the man *to see.*
> (adjective modifying man)

> Are you ready *to go?*
> (adverb modifying ready)

GERUNDS

Another verbal closely related to the infinitive is the **gerund.** Gerunds, like participles, end in *-ing.* They are always used as nouns. Here, in italics, are some examples:

> *Seeing* is *believing.*
> *Skating* requires good balance.
> The cliff was too steep for *climbing.*

PARTICIPLES AND
PARTICIPIAL PHRASES

The participle forms of regular verbs end in *-ing* (for the present participle) and in *-ed* (for the past participle). These forms may be used as adjectives: a *drenching* rain, a *cooked* goose.

Participial phrases are also used as adjectives. They are more complicated because, like the verbs they come from, they can have objects and be modified by adverbs. The entire phrase, with its object or its modifiers, serves as the adjective:

> *Frightened by the sound of the gunshot,* the rabbit scurried away. (Modifies *rabbit*)

> The dinner, *cooked to perfection,* was delightful. (Modifies *dinner*)

On a diagram, the participle is placed on a line like an adjective, but the line is bent to allow a place for the object of the participle, if it has one, or for modifiers:

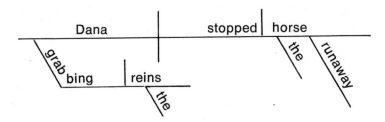

(Grabbing the reins, Dana stopped the runaway horse.)

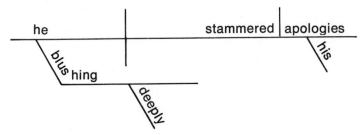

(Blushing deeply, he stammered his apologies.)

Diagrams are very helpful in dealing with participles and participial phrases because they require you to decide what noun or pronoun the participle modifies. By using diagrams, you won't fall into the trap of the **dangling participle.** Perhaps you have heard of that menace to good writing. A dangling participle is a participle that lacks a proper noun or pronoun to modify. Here's an example:

After studying the history of France all last night,
the exam turned out to be all about Germany.

The exam didn't do the studying, but the way the sentence is written, it sounds as though it did. The sentence should read:

After studying the history of France all last night,
I found that the exam was all about Germany.

Now the participial phrase modifies the pronoun *I*.

What happens when you try to make a diagram of the following sentences with dangling participles? Where do you place the italicized phrases?

Shouting vile curses, the warrior's spear
was thrown.

Standing on tiptoe, the parade could be seen.

I hope you gave up. It can't be done. But correctly rewritten, the sentences are easy to put into diagrams. Try it.

1. Shouting vile curses, the warrior threw his spear.
2. Standing on tiptoe, I could see the parade.

In the following sentences, find the participial phrases and decide what word or phrase they modify. How should each sentence be rewritten so that the meaning is clear?

1. Being in a hurry to finish my paper, several misspelled words weren't corrected.
2. Having painted the wall, my shoes were covered with paint.

3. Walking through the woods, the autumn leaves were in glorious display.
4. Working steadily, the carpenter's whole job was quickly finished.
5. Having missed several classes, the student's notes were incomplete.

Of course these sentences can be written correctly in several ways. The first sentence, for example, could be recast in this way:

> Since I was in a hurry to finish my paper,
> I didn't correct several misspelled words.

If you still have trouble with this, remember that the subject of the sentence should also be the doer of the participial phrase that precedes it.

Chapter 7.
The Mechanics of
Written Work

Speaking correctly is important if you want to make a good impression. But there are times when you'll have to show you can write English correctly as well.

Writing correct English is more difficult than speaking it. On the simple level of the sounds of words, it is hard for the ear to hear the difference between *should have gone* and *should of gone*. But written, one is clearly incorrect. Do you know which one?

There, their, and *they're* sound exactly alike, but when you write you need to remember which is which. (*They're going to put their coats over there* is a good sentence to practice writing if you have trouble with these homophones.)

Spelling is very important, but it is not discussed in this book. Here is a diagnostic test. If you have any difficulty in spotting the dozen spelling errors in the following paragraph, you need spelling help. Be sure to get it. There are many excellent self-help spelling books available.

You better watch you're dog. It dosent want too be tied on it's chain. Its two short. If it brakes the chain, you'll loose it and you won't no wear too find it.

Capitalization and punctuation are major writing problems too. Let's take a look at some of the rules in this area to follow and some of the traps to avoid. It won't be possible here to examine all the rules. There are just too many, and most are too familiar to merit discussion. You know, for example, that the first word in a sentence, in a quotation, in the greeting, or in the closing of a letter is always capitalized. You know that days of the week, months of the year, and names of holidays are capitalized. You've always used capital letters for proper names—the names of particular places, persons, groups, businesses, products, etc., so it's not necessary to stress these rules. Let's look, rather, at some situations that might be a bit more tricky:

Relationships
Words like father, uncle, and cousin are not capitalized unless they are used as part of a name:

> My dad told me to call you "Uncle Joe"
> even though you're not my uncle.

Directions
Compass points—east, west, etc.—are not capitalized unless they are used to refer to a region:

> We flew south to Atlanta because we had
> always wanted to visit the South.

School subjects
Names of school subjects like algebra and history are not capitalized, but names of particular courses are:

> She hasn't taken any history courses yet, so she
> was going to sign up for Medieval European History; unfortunately, it comes at the same hour as
> Biology I.

Seasons

Names of seasons—spring, summer, winter, and fall or autumn—are not capitalized.

Titles

All words in a title are capitalized except *a, an, the,* and short prepositions and conjunctions such as *in, to, and.* These words are capitalized, however, when they occur as the first word of the title.

Do you need some practice? Nothing has been capitalized in the following paragraph. Pick out the words that should be and list them on your paper:

> last wednesday in our earth science class, john was very embarrassed. he was thinking about the trip he was planning to take to visit his aunt and uncle in the east next winter. when the teacher called on him, he said, "yes, aunt helen?" everybody laughed.

There are a great many rules of punctuation, too many to set out here in detail. This is particularly true of the comma. See if you can discover some of these rules by noticing how commas are used in the examples below. Try to write a rule for each example and compare your answers with those in the answer key.

1. July 9, 1981. July, 1981.
2. Albany, New York. Paris, France.
3. Dear Joe, Sincerely yours,
4. Well, I'm going. Yes, I will. In fact, he's my brother. For example, seven is a prime number.
5. Mary, come here. Please, Mary, come here.
6. Our teacher, Mrs. Faulkner, is about to retire. Harold, who is the strongest boy on the team, will play quarterback.

Other uses of commas are mainly to help the reader separate ideas within a sentence. In long sentences a comma is used just before a conjunction or at the end of a participial phrase or an introductory adverb clause:

> Flying in the dark, the pilot relies
> on his instrument panel.

> When he flies in the dark, the pilot
> relies on his instrument panel.

> The pilot often has to fly in the dark,
> but he can rely on his instrument panel.

Commas are used to separate words in a series. They can often be indispensable for this purpose. Until you put the commas in where they belong in the following sentence, you won't know whether there were three or five items for lunch:

> For lunch they had cheese sandwiches
> chocolate cake and milk.

What was meant? Was it:

> cheese, sandwiches, chocolate, cake, and milk
> or
> cheese sandwiches, chocolate cake, and milk?

The best advice is: use a comma whenever it will help to make your meaning clear, but don't use them unnecessarily.

Chapter 8.
The Last Roundup

There are undoubtedly some problems you have encountered that haven't yet been mentioned. This chapter will try to round up some of these loose ends of good usage. Of course, there are many more than will be included here. But these are the ones that most frequently turn up in speaking and writing.

First, let's look at a group of common word pairs that sometimes cause confusion and that always seem to appear on language achievement tests.

Bring and Take
The key phrase to remember is "Take it away from me and don't bring it back to me." You *bring* something *toward* the speaker; you *take* it *somewhere else.*

Can and May
May I help you? (Will you give me permission?)
If you can. (If you're able to.)

Let and Leave
Leave him alone. (Go away, so that he has no one with him.)

Let him alone. (Don't disturb him.)
Let him make the signs. (Allow him to make them.)

Who, Which, That

When in doubt, use *that*. *That* can refer to people or things: the girl *that* I knew, the bell *that* I heard.

Which refers only to things.

Who refers to people or sometimes animals, if they're pets with proper names.

Who and Whom

Who is a subject pronoun—whether it's used as a relative pronoun (along with *that* and *which*) or as an interrogative pronoun (asking "Which person?"). *Whom* is an object pronoun in both situations. So use *who* wherever you'd use *he* or *she,* and use *whom* wherever you'd use *him* or *her.* This works well for longer clauses and wherever the pronoun follows immediately after the preposition:

This is the instructor *from whom* I learned so much.
This is the instructor *who* taught me so much.

The simple diagram for the object of the preposition looks like this:

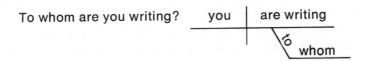

It's clear that you can't put a subject pronoun on the line after the preposition.

However, in ordinary informal speech, *who* has taken over completely when the sentence is reversed. Almost everyone now says "Who are you writing to?" and "Who are you talking about?" These usages are acceptable, however illogical they may be. They're in a class with "Aren't I?" and "It's me."

Sometimes people who are trying especially hard to use

the correct grammatical form at all times fall into the oppo-site trap—they use *whom* when *who* would be appropriate. Consider these sentences:

> I don't know if *he* is coming.
> I don't know if I should invite *him.*

There's no problem about the use of *he* and *him,* is there? Then consider these:

> I don't know _____ is coming.
> I don't know _____ to invite.

Which sentence needs *who* and which needs *whom*?

On a long distance call, the caller may say, "I'll speak to whoever answers." Is that correct? Yes it is. *Whoever* is short for "the person who." It is, therefore, the subject of the verb *answers,* not the object of the preposition *to.*

"Who did you say won?" Is that correct? Yes it is. *Who* is the subject of the verb *won. Did you say* is a parenthetical phrase, not part of the main sentence.

This and That, These and Those

This one is the one right here. So don't say *"this here* book," because you'd be saying "here" twice.

That one is somewhere else, somewhere over there. So don't say *"that there* book" for the same reason.

These is the plural of *this; those* is the plural of *that.* So it's *this kind* of sentence and *these kinds* of sentences. NEVER: *these kind* of sentences.

Who's and Whose

This is the same problem as *it's* and *its. Who's* means *who is*: Who's going? *Whose* means *belonging to whom*: Whose book is this?

We Boys and Us Girls

We is a subject pronoun and *us* is an object pronoun. This fact does not change by adding the words *boys* or *girls*.

We will do it.	Give us a chance.
We boys will do it.	Give us girls a chance.

Like and As

Like is a multi-purpose word. It can be a noun:

What are your likes and dislikes?

It can be a verb:

Do you like to ski?

It can be an adjective:

Jackets and pants are often made of like materials.

It can be a preposition:

He acts like a fool.
She looks like me.

What it can't be is a conjunction, even though people who write commercials like to ignore this fact. "Nobody can do it like MacDonald's can" may sell hamburgers, but it doesn't sell good English. Correct usage would require the commercial to say "Nobody can do it *as* MacDonald's can." It's "He looks as if he's scared," not "He looks like he's scared." Some dictionaries list *like* as a conjunction. But its use is still not really acceptable in formal speech.

Now here's a chance to see what you have learned thus far. On your paper, write the following sentences, choosing the correct word from the parentheses.

1. _____ (Take, Bring) your report card home and _____ (take, bring) it back in tomorrow.
2. _____ (May, Can) I have your address?

3. _____ (Let, Leave) sleeping dogs lie.
4. This is the young man _____ (who, which) is going to lead the tour.
5. He is the person _____ (who, whom) told you that.
6. I thought your brother was the one _____ (who, whom) they chose.
7. I can't imagine _____ (who, whom) told you that.
8. Do you like _____ (that, those) kind of mystery story?
9. Do you know _____ (who's, whose) house that is?
10. I'm sure that _____ (we, us) girls can run six miles.

Now let's deal with **misplaced modifiers** and other kinds of sloppy writing habits, best illustrated by these examples:

1) Mrs. Green gave Dorrie her first doll.

(Was it Mrs. Green's first doll or was it Dorrie's?)

2) Consider the placement of the word *only* in these three sentences:

Only English is spoken here.
(No other language is spoken here.)

English is *only* spoken here.
(Spoken but not written.)

English is spoken *only* here.
(This is the only place it is.)

Where would you put the word *only* in the following sentence to show that John didn't hit George in the stomach:

John hit George in the mouth.

Where would you put it to show that nobody but John hit George?

3) Classified ad:

WANTED TO BUY: typewriter desk
for student with folding legs.

(Folding at the knee or the ankle?)

4) Sitting here on the beach, looking out at the ocean, school seems years away.

(Why is the school sitting on the beach?)

5) His final mark of B+, after receiving failing marks all term, was a pleasant surprise.

(Did the B+ fail all year?)

6) I've been planning to visit my cousin for over a year.

(Are you sure you won't be outstaying your welcome? Wouldn't a shorter visit, maybe two or three days, be more reasonable?)

7) Last year I went to visit the house where I was born with my best friend.

(What an amazing coincidence that you two were born together.)

8) At the age of eighty-five I find that Mr. Butler has amazing vitality.

(Good for you. You don't look a day over 80!)

9) While on the telephone, the roast overcooked.

(A strange place to cook a roast!)

10) She draped her jacket over the chair so it wouldn't need ironing.

(A permanent-press chair?)

11) When photographing young children, the sun should not shine in their eyes.

(Who needs a camera? The sun will take the photo.)

12) I drove out into the country to see the leaves turning with my sister.

(What shade was your sister turning?)

What would you do to improve that dirty dozen? Revise these sentences and compare your answers with those suggested in the answer key.

"I MEAN, YOU KNOW AND ALL THAT JAZZ"

I mean, you know, it's gross. Right?

Don't be a boring speaker, someone who uses the same words and phrases over and over. Are you tired of the "new and improved" of TV commercials? Are you a bit skeptical of all the things that are touted as "terrific," "fantastic," "neat," and "super"?

Ask your friends to start counting how many times you say "I mean" and "you know" in the course of a day. You might find it's quite a lot.

You can wear out words as quickly as you can wear out your welcome. Be careful. Keep your language fresh and your grammar straight.

Answer Key

CHAPTER 1.

p. 3

1. This secret is just between you and *me.*
2. *We* girls are the best players.
3. They act *as if* they own the place.
4. My mother works in the library.
5. What do you think of this book?
6. Where did you hide it?
7. That engine doesn't start *as* it should.
8. Speak *more slowly.*
9. He can't see too *well.*
10. I can hardly hear you.
11. I don't know *anything* about it. (or I know nothing . . .)
12. Do you like to *lie* on the beach?
13. *Let* him be.
14. The radio *doesn't* work.
15. My brother and *I* will go to the fair.

CHAPTER 2.

pp. 6 to 7

subject	predicate
a. (I) or (she) or any noun or pronoun	never saw a purple cow
b. (You) or any noun or pronoun	(did) a splendid piece of work

OR

A splendid piece of work (won the prize)

c. (You)	go home
d. He	eats too much
e. (You)	never say die

p. 7

	ss	sp
1.	men	fought
2.	squirrel	tried

p. 11

complex sentence	main clause	subordinate clause
1	I wouldn't have	if I had
5	I won't let	unless you promise
8	will you buy	since you're waiting
compound sentence	conjunction +	
4	but they were	
7	or I'll never	
compound subject		
2	my friend George and my brother	
6	the basketball team and the football team	
compound predicate		
3	won and became	

CHAPTER 3.

p. 14

1. subject: athletes   direct object: medals

athletes | win | medals

2. subject: athletes   subject complement: celebrities

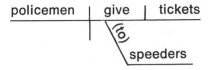

athletes | are \ celebrities

3. subject: policemen   direct object: tickets
                indirect object: speeders

policemen | give | tickets
          \ (to)
           \ speeders

4. subject: dogs   direct object: squirrels

dogs | chase | squirrels

p. 15
1. he
2. her   me
3. they
4. me
5. she

p. 16
1.

he
 \and
I /   ate | chocolate

2.

principal | gave | certificates
          \ (to)
           them
           \and
            us

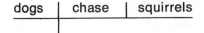

3.

she
 \and   Joe
he / phoned   \and
                me

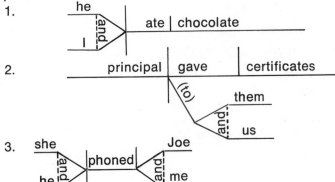

CHAPTER 4.

p. 20
1. action   stay

2. linking   is
3. linking   is
4. action   sample
5. linking   is
6. linking   is
7. linking   is
8. action   touch
9. action   establish
10. action   stares
11. linking   is

pp. 20 to 21
1. talk   (a)V. (b)N.
2. swimming   (a)V. (b)N.
3. dance   (a)N. (b)V.
4. walk   (a)V. (b)N.
5. help   (a)V. (b)N.

p. 21
Dogs bite.
Rover bit the deliveryman's leg.

She sings well.
What arias can she sing?

You can wash in the brook.
If you wash the dishes, I'll dry them.

They're winning!
I won a medal.

This car runs well.
She runs her father's business.

p. 24
1. has become   6. forgave
2. began   7. has stolen
3. have ridden   8. has drunk
4. has driven   9. threw
5. brought   10. have flown

p. 25

1. lying
2. lay your coat
3. lying
4. lain
5. laid them

6. laid two eggs
7. lie
8. lay
9. laid the cornerstone
10. lay me

p. 27
1. Each of the cats is going to catch a mouse for its dinner.
2. Neither of the men wants to change his vote.
3. Will either of the girls give up her place in the line?
4. One of the books has been moved from its proper place on the shelf.
5. Some of the books have been shortened for their reprinting in *Reader's Digest.*

CHAPTER 5.

p. 31

p. 32

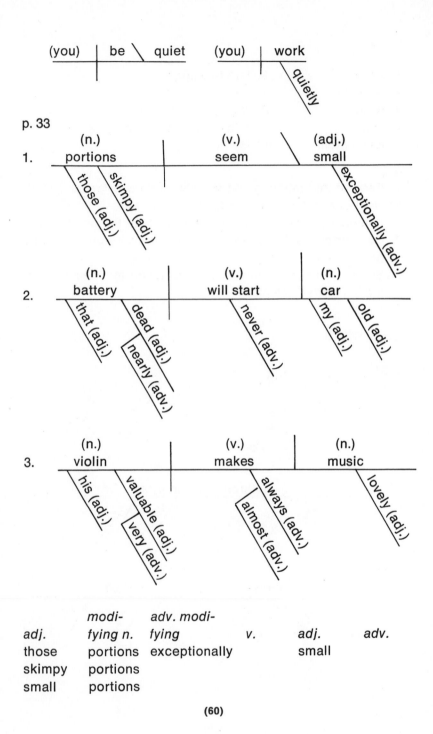

(you) | be \ quiet   (you) | work \ quietly

p. 33

1. (n.) portions | (v.) seem \ (adj.) small
those (adj.) skimpy (adj.) exceptionally (adv.)

2. (n.) battery | (v.) will start | (n.) car
that (adj.) dead (adj.) nearly (adv.) never (adv.) my (adj.) old (adj.)

3. (n.) violin | (v.) makes | (n.) music
his (adj.) valuable (adj.) very (adv.) almost (adv.) always (adv.) lovely (adj.)

adj.	modi-fying n.	adv. modi-fying	v.	adj.	adv.
those	portions	exceptionally		small	
skimpy	portions				
small	portions				

(60)

that	battery	never	start	
dead	battery	nearly		dead
old	car			

his	violin	very	valuable	
valuable	violin	almost		always
lovely	music	always	makes	

p. 35

1. I don't know anyone here.

       or

  I know no one here.

2. They don't know anything about it.

       or

  They know nothing about it.

3. The newborn colt can barely stand up.

4. We didn't have any money.

       or

  We had no money.

5. I can hardly hear you.

6. She never told anybody.

p. 36

1. taller
2. worse   worst
3. better   best
4. less   least
5. more slowly   most slowly

CHAPTER 6.

p. 38

1. of the sinking ship   aboard the remaining lifeboats

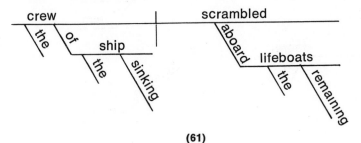

2. around the old playground   by the heavy storm

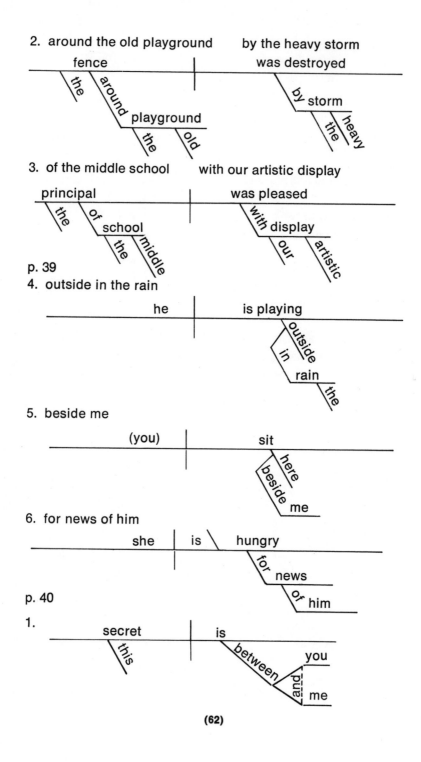

3. of the middle school   with our artistic display

p. 39

4. outside in the rain

5. beside me

6. for news of him

p. 40

1.

2.

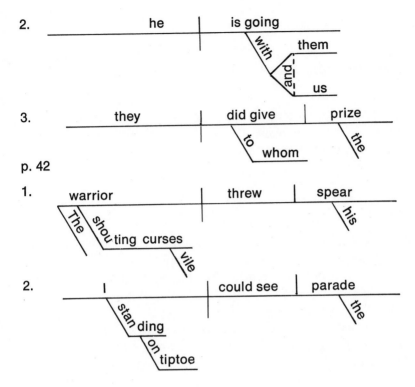

3.

p. 42

1.

2.

pp. 42 to 43
1. Being in a hurry to finish my paper, I left several misspelled words uncorrected.

                    or

   I neglected to correct several misspelled words.
2. Having painted the wall, I discovered my shoes were
   covered with paint.
3. Walking through the woods, we saw that the autumn
   leaves were in glorious display.
4. Working steadily, the carpenter quickly finished the whole
   job.
5. Having missed several classes the student realized that
   his notes were incomplete.

                    or

   he had incomplete notes.

CHAPTER 7.

p. 44
should have gone is correct

pp. 44 to 45
You'd better watch *your* dog. It *doesn't* want *to* be tied on *its* chain. *It's too* short. If it *breaks* the chain, you'll *lose* it and you won't *know where to* find it.

p. 46
Last   Wednesday   John   He   East
When   Yes   Aunt Helen   Everybody

1. Between parts of a date, but not between month and day.
2. Between city and state, city and country.
3. After a greeting and after the closing in a letter.
4. After introductory words that are not part of the main structure of a sentence.
5. and 6. To set off a word or phrase (called the appositive) or a relative clause that describes a person or thing and that could be omitted from the sentence without greatly changing the sentence's meaning.

CHAPTER 8.

p. 50
who is coming
whom to invite

pp. 51 to 52
1. Take   bring
2. May
3. Let
4. who
5. who
6. whom
7. who
8. that
9. whose
10. we

pp. 52 to 54
The following are only suggested revisions. There are other possibilities, equally good.

1. Mrs. Green gave Dorrie the first doll Dorrie ever had.
   or (if that was not what was meant)
   Mrs. Green gave her first doll to Dorrie.
2. John hit George only in the mouth.
   Only John hit George in the mouth.
3. WANTED TO BUY: typewriter desk with folding legs for student use.
4. Sitting here on the beach, looking out at the ocean, I feel that school is years away.
5. After receiving failing marks all term, he was pleasantly surprised by his final mark of B+.
6. I've been planning for over a year to visit my cousin.
7. Last year I went with my best friend to visit the house where I was born.
8. I find that Mr. Butler has amazing vitality for a man of eighty-five.
9. While I was on the telephone, the roast overcooked.
10. To avoid having to iron her jacket, she draped it over the chair.
11. When photographing young children, make sure that the sun is not shining in their eyes.
12. I drove out into the country with my sister to see the leaves turning.

Index